100 STEPS TO DOABLE

Pocket-Sized Inspiration to Make it Rain

Karen B. Kahn, EdD, PCC

Briggs
Publishing
Westport, Connecticut

100 Steps to DOable

Pocket-Sized Inspiration to Make It Rain
Karen B. Kahn, EdD, PCC

Published by Briggs Publishing,
Westport, Connecticut

Briggs
Publishing

Copyright ©2018 Karen B. Kahn
All rights reserved.

Cover and Interior design: Davis Creative, www.DavisCreative.com

Library of Congress Control Number: 2018906455

ISBNs: 978-0-9861100-2-3 (paperback)

            978-0-9861100-3-0 (Kindle)

            978-0-9861100-4-7 (ePub)

Quantity discounts are available on bulk purchases of this book for educational, gift purposes, or as premiums for increasing magazine subscriptions or renewals. Special books or book excerpts can also be created to fit specific needs. For information, please contact Briggs Publishing, 15 Danbury Avenue, Westport, CT 06880; phone: 512-250-8546 or email the author at Karen@ThresholdAdvisors.com

To all those who believe and behave with the following spirit in mind:

Success is a team sport. You don't have to know all the answers and you don't have to pretend you do. Anything you want to achieve is going to take the commitment of other people – and you can't buy commitment. No amount of money can buy loyalty. It takes commitment and loyal people who are inspired by a vision and want to contribute their talents to see a shared enterprise advance.

–Simon Sinek

Table of Contents

Introduction

I believe success and fulfillment is DOable. It doesn't always come in the form we imagine it, but with creative, smart thinking it IS achievable. This must have been ingrained in me from my inception; a strange occurrence in some ways as I am an "early baby boomer," and female, yet born to parents who told me I could be anything I wanted. More than pushing me toward fame and millions, this hardwiring fostered a passionate desire to inspire my children and those around me to make their dreams happen.

Many bumps and bruises along the way, along with ideas from many authors and mentors, and being a pre-Title IX athlete, led me to discover that there is a strategy to achieving dreams and goals. Daunting to DOable is a game plan derived from failures, wins, and guidance. To knowledge and strategies add patience, inspiration, encouragement, and resilience, and you'll make it happen.

100 Steps to DOable is a compilation of 100 posts I've made on LinkedIn over the past two years titled Coaching Notes. The purpose of these notes is to talk, encourage, and share. Sitting in front of my computer with my morning coffee, I truly picture myself talking to a universe of people, all preparing for a busy day, all wanting a simple answer to the question, "What can I do today that will make a difference in my career?"

We all can use a daily nudge to keep moving forward. I hope these 100 tips provide you with new ingredients, ideas, and reminders that will make your goals a reality. Thank you for your "Likes," questions, and trust.

Overview of
The Daunting to DOable
Methodology

1

Career choices are never easy for most of us, especially when it comes to deciding how and where to spend time. There are several givens that accomplishing new or "bigger" things require:

- You must know what you want.

- You must realize that, for the most part, it's up to you to do what has to be done. Sponsors, mentors, coaches, friends, leaders—all of those people, at the end of the day, are tangential; helpful, but tangential. It is up to you.

- You will feel some degree of discomfort while you are taking action. I consider this good or motivating anxiety—welcome it as it signals growth. (Still not a fun feeling!)

- You will probably have to dedicate more time and, in many instances, money (investment) than you want. Sure, there are ways to manage time and people like me who can give you ideas on how to take some business development actions in 10 minutes a day (if this is your goal). Nevertheless, next steps usually take you out of your time-comfort zone. So, don't automatically decide to "move up."

Review the above, and other elements, as they come to you. After considering them and "buying in," take the plunge. Clear contemplation and understanding about what it takes to move ahead helps you navigate towards your goals effectively and frustration-free.

2

Think about your practice as having two key components—your practice expertise (the work you do) and your business development focus (where you spend your business development-limited time). You need both components to become a rainmaker. Review your career. If you were laser focused on one segment of the marketplace, WHAT would it be? Define WHAT career success looks like to you.

3

You all have taught me that being a lawyer, learning about all of the changing and complex laws, is monumentally difficult. And if that wasn't enough, on top of those concerns, you must now learn the business of law in order for most of you to achieve your personal definition of success. In many of my discussions, among the most confusing pieces of this puzzle is the "need" to conceptualize your practice as having two different components: your substantive area and your business development focus. In the beginning, it often seems like these two areas don't come together naturally. If you want to be a rainmaker, you want to attract all kinds of business, not just your own—so you must think as a generalist. When you are focusing on your utilization, you think specifically about your particular expertise. In business development today, knowing an industry (like the toy industry) will help you originate all kinds of legal work—maybe not <u>just</u> in your substantive area. In your substantive work, you are happy to help any client in any industry. So, it feels like a puzzle and, at times, uncomfortable. Yet this two-pronged focus is essential to expanding your reach.

4

Jot down all the "things" that you would need to move toward your What, such as new knowledge, experiences, skills, connections, and ideas. Perhaps you want to change your substantive expertise—what knowledge would you need? Perhaps you would like to be the firm's Managing Partner—what experiences would you need and who would you need to know? Put together a list of what you need to get what you want, again, doing your best to put to the side any thoughts of "impossibility." Let the list develop over time, adding new ideas as you think of them.

5

From a client: "The size of my practice hasn't changed in 15 years, and frankly was never that big. What can I do to move forward?" "Sales" language doesn't feel appropriate for professional services. But in order to move forward you must define your buyers—I call these your WHOs. Too many lawyers trust that clients will simply appear. That might have been the case 15 years ago, but it is no longer. Today you need to know your market—your buyers. The longer the list, the higher your likelihood of success.

6

Starting your WHOs list can be a daunting task. Here is a way to think about it: There are four Relationship Buckets from which you will cultivate business—Inside the Firm, Past and Current Clients, Personal and Professional Network, and Industry Focus. All buckets might not be relevant to you. Start by thinking of who you know, or would ideally like to know/work with, in each bucket. Action (The HOWs) will go from here.

7

Here is a mantra to guide your relationship-development activities: "The person with THE MOST SUSTAINED, VALUE-BASED relationships makes rain and advances." Note the words in caps. MOST reminds you that having a large number of relationships expands your reach. SUSTAINED is key as staying in touch with your relationships develops them and deepens them. VALUE-BASED refers to maintaining an awareness of the needs of those around you and making efforts to make their personal/professional lives better and help them move toward what is important to them.

8

Business relationships are built on trust and giving. Here are elements that can provide significant value: ideas, introductions, resources, information (what they might not know), and support. Go through your WHOs. What value can be given to them?

9

Are you achieving momentum? This is an important question as without it efforts seem empty. Here's a trick—don't quantify your business development activities based on acquiring a piece of business. Instead, when you add someone to your WHOs and each time you are in contact with someone, give yourself a point. Make a chart to track how you are doing. Research tells us that it takes 10-20 points of connections to acquire a piece of business. Quantifying your actions gives you concrete feedback that you are doing what it takes to move forward. Reward yourself for each 20 points.

Relationship Buckets:
Inside the Firm

10

Who do you enjoy, learn from, and/or find valuable inside your firm? It is important to learn as much as you can from colleagues in all offices, in all substantive areas, and at all levels of expertise. All have something to offer you. Consider their goals and their clients. How can you be the person others describe as someone they can count on and a colleague who is valuable and likeable? Make a list of 20-30 colleagues inside the firm you would most like to get to know, or know better, during the next few months. Next to their name, jot down points of commonality and ways you could be helpful to each other.

11

Utilization numbers are elemental for success. Beyond the nuts and bolts of each matter are valuable collegial relationships. These individuals can advance your career, provide opportunities, foster introductions, and create a positive "buzz" about you. Remember, it is critical to have an awareness of what others need, not just your own needs. A vibrant internal network fosters advancement and a fulfilling sense of community.

12

As you position yourself to expand relationships inside the firm, consider exploring connections on different floors and areas around the firm. Key to your conversations is asking what they are working on and offering ways to expand their efforts. Go beyond "if you ever need a 'xyz' lawyer, give me a call." That is too passive. Talk to them about key issues for their clients about which they may not know. Remember, getting to know people involves continual contact and authentic caring.

13

What value can you provide a very successful, experienced senior partner if you are more junior? Plenty! If your senior partners are like me, help them with social media. Post things that they have written. Announce their successes on LinkedIn. Talk to them about ways to get value from social media. In addition, remember they need to provide value to THEIR clients. Check their client list. Find news items or articles related to their clients. Here is an important suggestion: Ask how you can be helpful. Explain this isn't about billable hours, but about other heavy lifting issues—there are plenty.

14

Want to "prime" your business development pump? Have strategic conversations with your partners. Been there done that? Take a different approach. The competitive pressure on lawyers has caused many to narrow their focus: getting business before anyone else and guarding the relationship. Help these usually successful lawyers expand the way they think about opportunities. Talk about specific clients, specific issues, and specific ways to work together to expand work with clients. Do not leave it to others to figure out how to talk about hot issues in your practice area. Give partners two ways to pose questions to their clients that could reveal work in your area. Emphasize that you know they "own" the client and that your intent is to work alongside them.

15

Who are the clients of partners in other practice groups? What do you know that can help these clients? Talk to the relationship partner when you have a specific idea concerning a current issue. "I would love to be involved with 'xyz' client on labor and employment needs," is too vague. Instead, approach the relationship partner saying, "I did some research and noticed that 'xyz' client has (or is likely to have) 'abc' problem. I would be happy to help you explore this topic with them."

16

Recent research from Heidi Gardner at Harvard revealed data showing that attorneys, practice groups, and law firms that practice collaborative business development make more rain than those using the traditional, individualistic, model. SO, get on board. Take three colleagues with different practice areas out for a cup of coffee. Talk about the clients and ideal clients that you have in common. Talk about how you can work as a team to develop relationships by attending to a variety of needs. Move beyond yourself and make it rain.

17

Today, practice Cross-Selling 2.0: Collaboration. Find someone in a different practice group who works with a client to whom you believe you could provide value. Take the time to research that client and identify services you could provide that would address relevant needs. Make sure needs exist. This shows you to be in tune with the client and not just "pitching in a vacuum."

18

Actively approach your colleagues instead of using the traditional passive approach. A passive approach is characterized by generic statements such as, "If you ever need me I would be happy to help." The likelihood of being called is minimal. An active approach provides specific information about a partner's client(s) and needs that may be relevant to that client. In an active approach you offer to work with the partner to help him/her expand the relationship with your knowledge. Make your approaches to others tangible, specific, and valuable.

Relationship Buckets:
Past and Current Clients

19

Contact a client team with whom you have worked within the past year. Ask about the impact of the work you did together. What has happened since the matter that they might not have anticipated. Having spoken about the matter, the implications of the work, etc., expand the conversation to issues such as those occupying their current attention. Make sure you prepare for the conversation so you have something "newsy" to share, such as an industry trend, information about a competitor, a new idea, or a helpful resource. Ending with a "give" (not do they have work for you) is a perfect way to close a conversation.

20

Make a list of clients you have worked with over the past 3 years, whether or not you are the originating partner (add all to your WHOs list). For each client, think about what could be the next piece of work for them— either one that follows on what you did last time or issues that might be current inside or outside of your practice area. Reach out to the person you had the most contact with. Say you were thinking about them and wanted to know how things were going post matter. If you have any personal information that you learned during the course of the engagement, ask a question about it. Staying in touch with clients is important. Make sure you maintain an awareness of their career moves.

21

What do you know about your clients? Expanding work with existing clients is the best way to deepen relationships and get new business. BUT, don't ask them for work. This puts you in the category of being a vendor and not someone with whom they have an ongoing relationship. Keep a working knowledge of changes and events at the company. Keep a folder/journal and learn/collect info about them, such as their products, strategy/goals, financial performance, org chart, major competitors, industry sector, customer base, suppliers, leadership, and culture. Take time to put this together—the more you know, the more value you can offer and the better you are positioned to keep them informed about challenges and opportunities that could lead to legal work.

22

Simple, obvious, and worth remembering: Ask clients how they are and listen to the answer. If you get the usual "fine," probe more such as about holidays, family, etc. The deeper the relationship, based on your fund of knowledge, the higher the likelihood that you will continue to get business and, more importantly, be known as a good person.

23

When contacting former clients, think proactively. Imagine that they are so busy keeping up with what they have on their plates that they don't know what important issues might be apt to make them vulnerable or be opportunities. Knowing and sharing this information is one of the criteria of great business developers. Let clients know that your definition of great client service is asking them questions like, "Have you thought about …," and "Did you know …" Explain that keeping them abreast of relevant issues is important to you—that you do your best to go beyond being a "matter only" person.

24

Learn from your colleagues. One lawyer recently told me, "I used a 'snow day' to go through all of my old calendars and made a list of people I worked with at the start of my career until now. Then, I looked them up on LinkedIn. Wow, many have joined some great companies since way back when." Here's the great part of the story. "I contacted one of them just to catch up. Sure enough she said, 'How nice to hear from you. Can you look at a contract for me?'" It doesn't always work like this of course, but you never know. Up and coming lawyers— keep a list of all people on your matters now! Experienced lawyers—hit the time machine and make a list of all the people with whom you have worked since you began to practice.

25

What trade associations are your clients a part of? During each client call for the next few weeks, ask this question. Becoming an active part of an industry community is important. By collecting this data you will be able to determine which one(s) are best for you to join to meet colleagues with similar interests and needs.

Relationship Bucket: Personal/Professional Network

26

When was the last time you spoke to family members about what you do? If they think of you generically, as "a lawyer," then you haven't fully (and simply) explained what you do. Don't underestimate your family's capacity as connectors, even your children. It may not be as important for them to understand the intricacies of your work as it is who you want to be introduced to—and vice versa. This adds a wonderful additional layer to family conversations—helping each other advance careers and other pursuits that are important to each person. I will never forget a partner asking me if it "counted" that his sister-in-law was an EVP of a Fortune 100 company (an ideal client for him), or my own daughter telling me that she met a partner at a large law firm—"Should I tell her you are a coach who can help them?" she asked me. No matter the depth of your family's true understanding of what you do, such conversations allow families to get to know each other better.

27

Are you one of those people who has lots of connections/relationships but haven't seemed to get business from people with whom you socialize frequently? If this describes you, it is likely not the connections but your conversations with your connections that is the problem. Do a quick assessment. What do you know about the business of your closest connections? When friends ask how you are, do you tell them that you are "overwhelmed" and "exhausted?" If so, you haven't integrated business talk into your relationships and that is a loss. Make a list of people with whom you are close but haven't talked in depth about business. What needs do you believe they have that you or your firm could help them with? This may be your next chat.

28

Client question: "I have some great contacts that I have cultivated over the years but have not talked to in a while. How do I reach out to those people?" My answer: When in doubt be honest. Try, "It has been terribly long since we have been in touch. I want to reconnect. How are things going with..." Be specific when asking about how things are even if the question seems dated. The same client further asked how to find current addresses. A big part of business development is research. If you get a bounce back e-mail, check LinkedIn and Google. You don't have to be in touch with everyone at once. Do one a day. You will be surprised by the responses you receive.

29

Reconnecting with law school friends is an important activity, no matter how long ago you were in school. Research these connections, even ones with whom you weren't very close. See what they are doing. Send a note acknowledging that you haven't been in touch, and that you have decided to strengthen your network comprised of people who can help each other. Plus, you know they are working at 'xyz' and would love to exchange experiences. Then schedule a "virtual cup of coffee" or even convene a mini reunion with 3-5 law school friends. Focus on learning about each other's careers and helping each other.

30

Do you tend to ask, "How are you?" Why don't you try something different? Perhaps ask about work. Try, "How are things at work?" "What's exciting at work these days?" "What are you working on these days?" Here's the key—when they answer, listen, and follow up with more questions. You are not deposing them—you are being interested. It is critical to convey authentic caring. Experiment and note the response.

31

Great question from a LinkedIn colleague: "How do I know if I am overstepping a relationship with a friend or a professional?" Selling your services when no one has expressed a need is, in my view, overstepping. On the other hand, asking about what someone does, being curious to understand the details, challenges, areas they enjoy is showing curiosity and is appropriate. Also, asking how they are dealing with an issue you have heard about is fine. Discussing the nuts and bolts of their jobs, industry, company is conveying interest. Bottom line: when you are engaged in an exchange of knowledge and not leading with your own need, you are likely not pushing and overstepping.

32

Most of us seem especially concerned about sounding inauthentic with friends whose company has a legal need. Explore a solution this way: How do you offer assistance to a friend who needs something personal, like a doctor's referral? It's easy, right? You simply give them a name or volunteer to do some research and find some names. Try emulating the comfort of this personal conversation if a business need arises. For example, during a conversation you hear that your friend needs a lawyer for a contract dispute or to assist in the acquisition of a business? You will always sound authentic when your motivation is to truly help, no matter what the context.

Industry Focus

33

It is easy to feel scattered and not effective with your business development efforts. A major trend to consider that will create focus and be effective is having an industry concentration. This strategy is **not** to limit your billable work; of course you will say "yes" to whatever projects come to the door. However, since your business development/nonbillable hours are limited, knowing a lot about one industry and cultivating relationships within that industry community is an effective methodology. Many firms are focusing on industries such as energy, technology, health care, finance, advertising, retail, etc. Consider a slice within one of these areas.

34

All businesses must analyze their potential marketplace before moving forward. Watching Shark Tank will confirm this. Issues to consider include: Who most wants what you have to sell? Where are they located? What is important to them? You want to have a narrowly defined market so you can create messages that will interest and attract companies with whom you most want to work. As you consider this concept, include industries that need a variety of legal expertise (not just yours). Start with research; don't just jump in.

35

"Do I really need an industry focus? I like working with an array of industries." I hear this from many lawyers and totally understand the enjoyment of working with different businesses. However, it is important you understand that the legal marketplace has experienced vast changes since the early 2000s. Today, clients want you to understand their business and their industry. They want you to integrate legal solutions specifically into their business objectives. In addition, clients usually want people that they have gotten to know, with whom they have developed some trust. Developing the kind of relationships that foster trust and confidence requires many points of connection (some research says 10-20). Focus enables efficiency in the process. As one CMO said to me, "Unless you have enough time to get to know all of the players in five industries and can stay up to speed on the intricate ins and outs of many industries, then you must focus on one." Not only will this strategy help you, but it also helps your firm expand its overall relationship map.

36

Many elements go into choosing an industry focus. First, it must fit into the strategic objectives of the firm. What industries are important to the firm? How can you expand that footprint with your substantive knowledge? What subareas of that industry warrant expanded attention? The answer to these questions will make you valuable to the firm and enable you to utilize an established platform. Also consider what industry would be fun to be a part of. Working within a business community where you are interested in what they are doing makes business development fun.

37

For so many lawyers, having one business development focus is counterintuitive. After all, shouldn't you cast your "net" as wide as possible? But think of it mathematically—if you have limited time and it takes 10-20 points of connection to develop confidence in potential clients (knowledge about a client's industry is important), do you have time to focus on more than one industry? It's really not time efficient or effective to go outside of one sector with these odds, even though anxiety that you are missing someone with a matter will plague you! This leads to the question about how to choose the "right" industry sector. Here are some criteria to consider:

1) Is it an industry you will enjoy knowing about?

2) Does it have broad legal concerns (across several practice groups)?

3) Can they pay your rates?

4) Are there associations where people gather?

5) Are they geographically relevant to where you want to practice?

6) Is the industry connected to the firm's direction?

I have found that 200-300 potential clients in the sector is a good target number. With those components, if you work to construct a smart strategy in which you become a valuable part of the industry, over time, you will have plenty of work.

38

Put yourself in the position of an in-house counsel who is looking for a lawyer. She is considering two lawyers, both of whom she has vetted to have the substantive skills and knowledge she believes she needs. One has a track record of work and involvement with many companies similar to hers; one has broad experiences but only smatterings in her industry—who do you choose? In the current legal marketplace, with so many available firm lawyers, the choice for in-house counsel is usually the person with specific industry expertise, knowledge, and relationships. Having spoken with very many lawyers who have built their career on working across industries and, frankly enjoy that part of their work, I understand this is a difficult trend to embrace. It's not a matter of being able to work across industries—you can do that, I understand. Rather, it is positioning yourself to be most appealing. Your attractiveness increases when you can show that you understand clients' business objectives, the hot issues in their industries, how similar companies have approached similar challenges, etc. Before saying "no" to an industry focus, obtain some marketplace intelligence, explore particular industry segments, and contemplate what such a focus might be like for you.

39

Look at your firm's top industry group—technology, financial services, life sciences, energy, retail, etc. These are macro industries, too large to attend to as a business development strategy at large. Now ask yourself, which of these industries has the most need for your legal expertise/input now and in the future? With this information, slice off a piece of the industry for your attention such as retail technology, health care finance, midsize banks, etc. This creates a business focus for you and enables you to understand a particular clientele to become a true differentiator in this competitive market. First step? Research—you may be surprised what subgroups have created trade associations, conferences, and communications. This is a sign that you chose a viable direction. See what you discover.

40

An industry focus allows you to efficiently and effectively learn about a defined group of potential clients so you are well positioned to cultivate the kinds of knowledgeable and trusting relationships that lead to work. Research is key for becoming an industry expert. Gather articles that discuss trends in your industry focus. Some lawyers put these articles into a binder (or electronic folder) so they can read at their leisure. Reading provides important topics for conversation, questions, and writing. The more you know about what people in your selected industry are talking about the easier it is for you to become an integral and valuable member of the community.

Conference and Event Strategies

41

Going to conferences is an intimidating yet essential activity for lawyers—memories of high school dances where no one asks you to dance flood psyches, even if you were the king/queen of the prom. Why the trepidation? Because you see the event as a chaotic necessity and not a clear-cut opportunity. Having a strategy will move you from "hoping something great happens" to achieving specific goals. There are four steps to optimizing the potential of a conference or any gathering:

1) Preparation—knowing what you want to accomplish, researching who you want to meet, developing a clear message

2) Execution—navigating the event with purpose, engaging others authentically and valuably

3) Debrief—capturing all you learned

4) Follow-Up—compelling post-conference messages that builds upon conversations begun at the conference

Moving deliberately through these steps allows you to cut through the overwhelming chaos and make time spent rewarding.

42

Many of you are prepping for conferences, seminars, etc. Riddle: What is the purpose of conversations at conferences? Answer: To set up your next conversation. Fight the inclination to talk to someone for 30 minutes. Five- to ten-minute conversations that conclude with: "Let's continue this discussion next week," will allow you to maximize the very expensive face time potential you have with people. Set goals before you go: Who do you want to talk to?

Why are you going to the conference? Go from hoping this is a great conference to making it a great conference by knowing, up front, what you want to accomplish.

43

Preparing for Events #1—Why are you going to this conference? Most likely one of your responses is to meet people who can be valuable to you in some way, such as giving you a piece of business. Instead of going to the conference hoping (again that word) that you will meet key people, plan ahead.

1) Who would you, ideally, like to meet? Make a list.

2) Learn if those you would like to meet will be attending. This may be difficult. Try asking the conference organizers for a list of attendees; recalling (or asking a colleague) who attended last year; looking at

the list of speakers and sponsors. (When all else fails, go to the conference early and look at the table of name tags, but this won't help you in preparation.)

3) Reach out to as many people as you can ahead of time. Plan times to get together such as during networking time, sit together at lunch or at a break out session, meet for dinner, etc.

The more you plan ahead of time, the more you are taking "hope" out of your return on investment equation.

44

Preparing for Conferences #2—With your list in hand (from note above) prioritize your contacts. Create groups of five and assign them a priority—1st, 2nd, 3rd, etc. Each group represents this thinking: "If I can only connect with five people at the conference, these individuals are my first priorities." Now, research each individual. What do you want a conversation with each person to entail? Research current activities for them and their business. List five questions you will ask each person to explore his/her needs. Preparing conversations will make your connections more valuable for you and the other person.

45

Preparing for Conferences #3—Stop hoping conferences will be productive, make them productive by contacting your top-priority people ahead of time. Tell them you would like to make sure you connect and make a plan to sit next to them at a speaker, meet at the nametag desk, see each other during a break, etc. If you don't know the person, explain why connecting with them is important to you. This isn't a sale, this is a connection. State what you know about what they are working on and how it connects with your activities. Preparation increases your attendance ROI.

46

How do you talk about yourself at conferences? This is a sensitive question with a counter intuitive answer: don't lead with the fact that you are a lawyer—that shouldn't be your first sentence—perhaps your second. Rather, consider this—we live in a world of sound bites. This means that we have become programmed to listen to the first few words of a message and then we unconsciously decide whether to continue listening. So you must use the initial "sound real estate" wisely. Remember that one of your primary goals of attending conferences is to make connections. Therefore, make your first few words count. I suggest that the first words that describe yourself be a type of business with which you would like to garner work. Answer

"What do you do?" with "I work with large digital health companies." Typically you will get a retort like this: "Oh what do you do for them?" Now you have the person's attention and can say more such as: "As a lawyer, I help companies that are developing new surgical tech tools register their patents…" Note, you don't need to say the name of your firm—usually that does not register with a listener in a way that fosters further conversation. We are in a relationship-based marketplace—your goal is to start a relationship. After this initial intro, put the focus back on them. No need to impress.

47

Was that conference worth my time? Great question! The answer depends on whether you sustain the relationships you began. Debriefing your experience will help you capture all information and ideas you received at the conference. There are many areas to record. First, write down everyone with whom you spoke. The length of time you spoke isn't an issue. What did you learn about the person? Who wasn't there that could have benefitted from the experience? What did you learn substantively? Might you want to speak at next year's conference? Given your experience, what topics might have value? Thinking about all you met, learned and thought about contributes to the way you answer your question about whether the conference was worth your time.

48

Follow-up action determines the return on investment (ROI) of time at conferences. Some people counsel that if you aren't going to follow up, don't go to the event. Remember that the primary purpose of conference attendance is to begin or expand relationships. Crafty conference execution allows for many "touches." When the conference is over, the next step of sustaining those relationships begins. You want to continue every conversation. Ideally, during the discussion, you identified a need possessed by the other person. Follow up on topics—where they got their shoes, what they said about their company, something about a child or a hobby. The key is to keep a conversation going, especially providing something that responds to a need that was mentioned. Consider an introduction, resource, idea, or piece of information. Remember, the person with the MOST SUSTAINED, VALUE-Based relationships makes rain. Following up after conferences is a pathway to obtaining business and special relationships.

49

Many people have told me that if they aren't speaking at a conference they don't attend. This is a mistake. While raising your profile is valuable, I believe that a more expansive goal is to spend time with your WHOs. If you do homework ahead of time, make contact with key people and research issues that people at the conference will be interested in, the value of going is major. Set goals, make contacts, determine talking points about what is important. Have face time with people with whom you wouldn't be able to shake hands otherwise. If your WHOs are in the room, the value is significant.

50

You went to a conference/meeting and for a variety of reasons missed speaking to the people you wanted to see. Perhaps they didn't attend, maybe you were called out for a call or you just didn't find them. Don't panic. You can still reach out to them and start a conversation starting with, "I'm sorry that we didn't meet up at the conference." When you reach out, remember to be very clear about what you want to speak about, such as something critical that you learned at the conference, something you want to share or even a topic about which you would like to exchange ideas. Ask for a BRIEF telephone chat. Make sure you are clear about what the value of connection is to the person. Remember, just like you, they are busy.

Why Should I Do
Business Development?

51

I had a very moving meeting with a relatively new partner recently. It was similar to meetings I have had with others in comparable positions. This was the fourth coaching meeting she had and, despite giving herself homework at the end of each session, she had not followed through on her self-assigned tasks. What had she been doing? Things that were helping others at the firm and, of course, client work. She was dismayed and embarrassed. After assuring her that not having done "homework" wasn't a betrayal of our work, but conversely, an indication that we had yet to establish a clear beginning point for our work, she calmed down and focused. "I have spent my entire life reaching for goals established by others and now that I am a partner, I have no idea what I want." Prioritizing business development requires knowing YOUR definition of a MEANING-FULL career. This knowledge positions all of your actions and drives career motivation. At our next coaching session, the above woman and I spent time talking about what being a lawyer meant to her and what she wanted to accomplish in her life as a whole, personally and professionally. At the end, she assigned herself an important homework task: think about what she wants her career as a lawyer to bring into her life.

52

Potential Reason #1 to Engage in Business Development—Increase your INCOME. Obvious, right? What would an increase in income tangibly do for you? Pay off loans? Retirement savings? One client told me that she wanted to create a large fund for each of her children so that they would be able to receive all of the education they wanted in order to become happy, independent adults. Another client said that she was saving money so she could leave Big Law and become a high school teacher without changing her lifestyle. What would you do with more money? If Potential Reason #1 motivates you (which it might not), write down your dream expenditures on post-it notes. Post them where you can see them often, such as at the bottom of your computer monitor. Remember, this is what business development could bring into your life that is important to you.

53

Potential Reason #2 to Engage in Business Development—Freedom to create your IDEAL way of practicing law. Rainmakers are given the flexibility to determine how, what, and where they practice. When you are seen as valuable to the firm, you can work more from home; travel more to connect with clients; integrate more of your interests into your work; come in later in the day after a run, workout, time with the kids, etc. Business development fosters a "hands off" attitude towards how you practice. Does the idea of working YOUR way appeal to you? If so, this "potential reason" is a motivator. Write "IDEAL" on a post-it where you can see it and be reminded of this vision, especially on those days when you don't feel like reaching out to your network.

54

Potential Reason #3 to Engage in Business Development—The INDEPENDENCE to practice law anywhere you want, such as on your own, with a start-up boutique or another firm. A book of business and an extensive WHOs list gives you choices. This is particularly important should a downturn, merger/acquisition, or change of direction happen in your firm. With a "book," you will be wanted by the legal marketplace. Knowing that you have the power of independence often provides individuals with a sense of freedom, power, and happiness. If working independently is important to you, put "Independence" on a post it note to remind you to work towards this important value.

55

Potential Reason #4 to Engage in Business Development—Generating revenue for the firm gives you a seat at the table and ability to IMPACT the direction of the firm. Have you ever thought about changes you wish the firm would make: comp structure, ways colleagues work together, money spent on professional development, use of technology, etc.? The more you contribute to the firm's bottom line, the louder your voice becomes and the greater your position to create a firm that fits your values and ideas about best practices. If you are passionate at the thought of being able to make change, post IMPACT where you can see it of-ten, to remind you of this value and motivate you to attend to business development.

56

Potential Reason #5 to Engage in Business Development—Having a large book of business makes you INVULNERABLE (or less vulnerable) to the ups and downs of the marketplace, national economy, and overall firm stability. How often do you get a fleeting worry about your future at the firm? (Will they ask me to leave?) Those who generate business for the firm are needed no matter what. If you want some solace from the "middle of the night jitters," post INVULERABILITY where you can see it. This will serve as a reminder that taking actions that lead to business generation will help you keep your roots solidly planted at the firm.

57

Potential Reason #6 to Engage in Business Development—You work hard, and every once in a while you know you deserve a treat—INDULGE. When you have a substantial book of business you can set aside an allowance for yourself. It might be for a monthly massage, an art lesson, special outfit, or a trip. If "rewarding yourself" for the time and energy spent on your career would add fulfillment into your life, write INDULGE on a piece of paper and post it where the image of having/doing something fun for yourself will spur you towards forming valuable relationships that may lead to business.

Forming Valuable Relationships—
Some HOWs

58

Listen for needs of others with the ears of a generalist, not just about your area of expertise. Try this question when talking to others, "What are you most excited about doing at work these days?" Ask follow-up questions until you have an idea about how the person succeeds (not just with legal knowledge). Focusing on an individual's "personal side" is also an important direction for inquiry. Ask "What are you most excited about this spring?" Awareness of needs leads to the development of deeper relationships.

58

Relationships thrive on reciprocity. I can't say this to you loudly enough. Last week, someone I have known for a relatively short period of time, introduced me to someone very valuable to me—I didn't even ask for the intro. I was so touched and appreciative. I am now strongly motivated to go the next mile in return. If you believe, like I do, that the key to success is expanding who you know, then creating a network that is based on vibrant giving among members is an important goal to pursue.

60

Here is the most powerful way to establish or deepen a relationship: Ask, "How can I help you?" You can expand the question by asking, "Is there anyone I might know, or information that I might have that can help you advance to your goals?" Change the wording to fit your style, keeping the spirit of helping in mind. People who ask this question show their true nature through action.

61

I obtained one of my guiding principles for sustaining relationships from MSNBC commentator, Chris Matthews, who often asks his panel: "Tell me something I don't know." Utilizing this philosophy makes you valuable and proactive. Stay on top of business trends, current events, and legal news. This time investment makes people look forward to seeing you and gives you information that keeps conversations fresh and relevant.

62

Add this simple question to your conversation toolbox: "How are you doing with …" This inquiry should be about something outside of your current work with a person. Fill in the blank with something that taps into an important topic, trend, issue, person, or company they might not have thought about for a while or is a "hot topic" that might be impacting their work. For example, with a senior partner, you might ask about a client they are currently working with who might be grappling with an issue outside of the partner's area of expertise. For a client, ask about a regulation change or a topic that has recently been in the media.

63

The most frequent question I am asked is: "How do I make THE ASK?" There is a lot of confusion and debate on this topic contributing to "business development anxiety." Every rainmaker and rainmaking coach will give you a different answer. Listen to all of them and see what fits for you. Here is mine: business development in professional services companies happens in the context of two elements—a trusted relationship and when there is a need. Unless there is an emergency, people don't "impulse buy" lawyers like they might an article of clothing. I see most "asks" as coming from an individual's need for business, not the other person's need for a solution or assistance. Instead of asking people for work in the same tone as asking about the weather, OFFER assistance when a specific issue is revealed. This gives your conversation context and keeps the focus on them. I find this to be relationship enhancing and respectful.

64

In further pursuit of insight about THE ASK, I asked some in-house counsel how they felt when a direct "out of the blue" ask is made. "I hate it when they ask when I haven't stated a need for a lawyer. It is so awkward. I know they want business. I will ask for their services when I need or want to." Wanting to establish a positive note, I followed up with what kind of business conversations they preferred to THE ASK. "Tell me something I might not have thought about or know. If we need this, I will ask." Great advice. Punch line—don't ASK. Replace this approach with being knowledgeable about what might be relevant to others.

65

Suggestion from a rainmaker: Apply the '6 foot' rule at all times. By this she means, know everyone within 6 feet of you. This doesn't mean grilling people or trolling for business at the beach (but this attorney does have powerful conversation on chair lifts!). What it does mean is maintaining an awareness about people around you and displaying curiosity about what they do, their interests, and their lives. "You never know," this rainmaker told me, the person next to you at one of your children's graduation could be the CEO of a major company."

66

In our hurry-up culture we often default to "cutting to the chase" in our conversations. Perhaps this saves time—I'm not sure about this but it feels like it does—but it eliminates the opportunity to deepen a relationship. When I say "deepen," I don't mean you need to have an extensive discussion. However, asking a question about how work (or their life in general) is going and then actually listening to the answer strengthens bonds. Go beyond being "just" a good lawyer to being a lawyer people really enjoy working with. Not only will this brand increase the likelihood that you will get continuous work, but, let's cut to the chase, it will show you to be a true, caring, human being.

67

"Do I need to go out for dinner every night in order to be a great rainmaker?" Great question that I receive from many clients. Absolutely not! Everyone is busy these days. And, to tell you the truth, I think most clients don't really want to go out to dinner with you every night either. Short, valuable face time can be had at conferences and other, briefer, contexts. That being said, we are fortunate, these days, to have many ways to be in touch with people. These modalities, with practice, can be just as effective in creating substantial relationships as the traditional tools. It is worth your time to learn to craft "connective" e-mail conversations that have humor, warmth, and personality. Practice—ask colleagues (or your coach) for feedback until you develop your friendly, yet still professional, e-mail voice.

Tackling Time Challenges

68

Making rain is not a big deal—it is a series of small, daily actions that you can even do while engaged in fun activities during a weekend. Ask yourself what you can willingly say "yes" to doing this week. Consider talking with someone about his/her work; reading a business magazine to find an article to send to someone; gazing at a website of a past/current client to learn how they talk about their business. Daily "small" actions produce momentum. All "count" and will move you forward.

69

Busy time, lots of hours, "Sorry coach, no time for business development." I hear this a lot and want to help you to not get caught in that trap.

No matter how busy you are, take five minutes—only five minutes—to think, reach out to, or read about a potential client. Set a time—don't worry about doing this five-minute "drill" perfectly. Here is a list of brief actions to consider:

1) Day one—Make a list of five people (best if they are in the same industry) you would like to be in touch with.

2) Day two (remember don't spend more than five minutes)—Look for an article that would be interesting and relevant to all five.

3) Day three—Write three sentences explaining why this article might be interesting to them.

4) Days four and five—Send the article to all five. Each one must have two sentences in the beginning that are personal to the individual.

Great job—in one week, you have connected with five valuable people.

70

Here is a game plan for business development action:

1) SELECT someone from your WHOs list

2) EXPLORE your notes about them across four areas (Family, Occupation, Recreation, Desires)

3) ENGAGE by e-mail, phone, or in person

Keep your focus on creating long-term value for them. You don't need to impress, sell, entice—just offer something related to what is important to them. Finally, monitor your expectations. You might or might not hear anything back from the selected individual. That is fine—count your actions, not responses.

71

Try a five-minute drill related to the personal/social part of your network, specifically, friends/acquaintances you likely know well but with whom you have never talked about business or careers. Stop and don't think "ASK for business." Instead, use the game plan below:

1) SELECT the person.

2) EXPLORE/IDENTIFY NEEDS by spending three minutes on the person's business website.

3) THINK about what kinds of issues similar organizations are dealing with AND what are the person's professional goals. If you don't know, tee up that question.

4) ENGAGE by calling the person and setting up a one-on-one time that is professionally focused. "You know, we spend so much time talking about our kids (or

being focused at the gym, yoga studio, art lecture, etc.) that we have never talked about our work. I would love to have a quiet drink and chat about how we spend most of our waking time." Perhaps you don't have to go into that kind of buildup. If not, just call, set up drinks, and have a professional talk.

Feel strange? Think of it this way: the more we find ways to help each other and those important to each other in all aspects of life, the better the world is. Set a time to expand aspects of your relationships.

72

Here is a five-minute drill that addresses the "I got a call out of the blue" phenomenon. If the call is truly a surprise realize that there are opportunities out there to which you are relying on "luck" to bring your way. To remedy this:

1) SELECT someone who you did some work with over the past two years.

2) EXPLORE by recalling what you did for the person, how the project was important to their work and anything you might have discussed outside of the matter.

3) ENGAGE by writing a note asking about the lasting impact of what you did. Did they still find the work helpful? Ask about personal information you learned during the time you spent together. In the body of the e-mail, include a personal or professional question—this tends to encourage a reply. Don't worry if you hear back, just give yourself "credit" for engaging.

73

I'm often asked about business development time savers. The best one I know is to have a structure. While it may take time to create a relationship list (WHOs List), it will save you a lot of time later on. I believe that Excel is the best format as it allows you to create fields (such as geography, industry, type of relationship, etc). Break up this project into five-minute tasks. Consider one category at a time, such as individuals from each of the following Relationship Buckets: Inside the Firm; Past and Current Clients; Personal/Professional Relationships; and Specific Industry Members. Of course, there are other subcategories such as law school friends, family, neighbors, etc. If you spend five minutes a day, I bet you will have 50 names by the end of a week.

74

Knowledge is power. It positions you as someone who is relevant and valuable. But who has time to read everything that would be ideal? No one! Get a few colleagues from all levels of experience and split up resources in which interesting information may appear. It is important that each individual share what kind of information would be helpful to him/her such as articles about an industry or area of interest. When key articles are found they must be given to the appropriate person. Having a team expands each individual's ability to search and find relevant material for those with whom they want to provide value and stay top of mind.

Core Ideas to Keep in Mind:
Rainmaking by the Numbers

75

Success in law firms requires the acquisition of two components (one is not enough):

1) Strong area of legal expertise

2) Large network of value-based relationships

76

The strategy for making rain and relationships has three steps that must be followed in sequence:

1) WHAT do I want to accomplish in my practice?

2) WHO can help me get there?

3) HOW can I form lasting, valuable relationships with my WHOs?

77

There are **two-and-a-half** categories of WHOs:

1) BUYERS (or users) of legal services or other things that I want

2) CONNECTORS to the above

3) HYBRID of both (this is the .5)

78

WHOs are spread among **four** "buckets":

1) INSIDE your firm or organization

2) CLIENTS past or current on whose matters you have worked

3) PERSONAL and PROFESSIONAL network

4) INDUSTRY or GEOGRAPHIC focus

79

There are **three** vehicles to use to sustain relationships:

1) E-MAIL, which can take as little as 60 minutes to provide value

2) TELEPHONE, which takes a minimum 10-15 minutes in order to be interpersonally effective

3) IN-PERSON, which is typically the most time consuming

80

Relationship development involves learning about four aspects of an individual:

1) **F**AMILY—people who they consider family

2) **O**CCUPATION—job-related information

3) **R**ECREATION—what they do for fun

4) **D**REAMS—aspirations

Note, the above spells FORD, like the car.

Extra Tips for Success

81

Not making progress in biz dev? There is a method to the madness of the rainmaking game. Here are some questions to ask yourself:

1) Are you expecting relationships to yield business too quickly/unrealistically? Relationships need time to develop. Ultimately, people will work with you when they have developed trust and confidence in you and see you as someone who cares about THEIR business.

2) Do you understand their business? Just being a good lawyer is not enough anymore. You must convey at all times that you understand their business, direction, industry, challenges, etc.

3) Are you selling in a vacuum? Remember, business only comes when there is a need. If they don't need your services, they won't (can't) engage your services.

4) Are you organized? Do you have a business development strategy? Do you have a clear direction? Have you defined your "ideal client?" Take time to analyze. When you reflect on what you are doing you can make adjustments.

82

The key to success as a rainmaker is taking the time to organize. If you describe your relationship-development activities (no matter what your level of expertise) as "scattered," you will not succeed significantly. If you are darting around, blogging, going to meetings, having lunch with people, speaking, etc., with no clear direction, stop and think specifically about what you want to accomplish. Run your ideas by a colleague or a business development professional. Be open to feedback. Investing time in a clear direction will serve you career-long.

83

Success occurs when your approach fits your personality, comfort zone, values, and goals. One lawyer constructed a chart with tiers: Tier 5 is made up of companies with relationships she knows very well. She is their go-to lawyer. Tier 4 is made up of companies that she knows well- they give her some work but not for "all" their legal needs. Tier 3 is made up of companies in which she has done one piece of work. Tier 2 is composed of companies where she knows at least one person but has ever worked for them. Tier 1 lists companies that fit her definition of "ideal client" but she doesn't know anyone who works there. She finds this structure helps her prioritize action.

84

The key to business development is having strong, sustained relationships. Monday, select 10 individuals with whom you want to connect. Send a note that provides relevant information or connects to a prior discussion. Don't worry if you hear back, you have no control over that and, as we know, people are busy and have to choose where to put time. Your overarching goal is to consistently, build and strengthen relationships through providing thoughtful communications. Keep a record of your messages so you can keep track of your consistency.

85

Start all e-mails with a "connective remark"—something that is personal or is in some way relevant to the ongoing relationship. Then, as needed, move on to your agenda. Remember, your goal is to create strong, ongoing, valuable relationships. This means you must connect, not just "do." Keep communications short yet warm.

86

Spend small bits of time gathering valuable information that you can send to people. Get magazines such as Bloomberg Business, Fast Company, Inc, Wired, etc. Glance at the business sections of Sunday newspapers (at least) and note information from the internet. When you send information include a note about why the article is relevant, such as it is an example of something they are dealing with; an important trend; something about a competitor; about a personal interest. Don't put "fyi" in the subject line or as the only note in the e-mail. Show you respect the other person's time by giving them information up front.

87

"Calendaring" appointments with yourself to attend to business development increases the likelihood that you will take action and gain momentum. Even if you cordon off five minutes, schedule a time and keep the appointment.

88

Do you call yourself a "complex commercial litigator?" This doesn't mean enough to potential buyers—it is way too vague. Many lawyers who identify themselves with this label do so to reflect their breadth of substantive knowledge and experiences. They also want to make sure they obtain as many opportunities as possible. Yet, as strange as it may sound, in the current business development climate, you will attract more work by being more specific about what you do and who you tend to serve. For example, choose a characterization of yourself that describes the kinds of problems you can address and an industry you know a lot about. As counter-intuitive as it may sound--the narrower your focus, the more business you will attract.

89

Take time to put a personal note on business e-mails. Connect to something that is going on in the client's business, industry in general, or personal life. This makes you a human lawyer, not an impersonal vendor. Yes, it takes an extra minute to create something, but forging these connections strengthens relationships and plants roots for future conversations.

90

Business development does not take the intensive focus required of legal work. Therefore, double dip—do activities required to sustain relationships while you are doing something else. Since I watch television the "old fashioned way" (there are commercials), I send e-mails during the breaks. If you have school-age children, do your business development "homework" while they do theirs; even do some quick reading in between errands. Most important, no matter how complicated life seems, inserting five minutes of action on a daily basis clears the important pathway for success. It is DOable.

91

Introvert. "I'm an introvert and not comfortable at conferences. How can I make conferences productive for me?" So you're an introvert—most lawyers are. This doesn't mean you can't be a rainmaker—we just need to orient circumstances to you. The obvious: you don't like networking events. Large events are an efficient use of time, however, unlike the extroverts, you get tired of having multiple conversations quickly. Therefore, you must plan ahead. Who do you want to speak with? What do you want to talk about? Reach out ahead of time, if you can. At events have a 10-minute conversation and then agree to continue via phone. How many can you handle before you get exhausted? Set that number. Complete your "assignment" and then you are done. You will be more comfortable if you can take a person to the side to speak as opposed to being in a small group. Rely more on e-mail conversations—yes they work. Think about this: I am most comfortable talking to people under "x" circumstances—make a setting fit what is best for you. Don't worry if you don't know as many people as your extroverted colleagues. Know who you want to meet for business development (in or outside of conferences) and focus on those. It's not quantity, it is the quality (and sustainability) of the conversations that matters. It's DOable, just your way.

92

Motivation. "I just don't like the notion of business development. How can I get myself to do it?" I see motivation as having two components: Big Picture (what is really important to you) and Daily Picture (how to keep your goals front of mind and constantly moving forward). For most people, developing business in itself is not intrinsically motivating—it's not fun, stimulating, or interesting. However, it IS a pathway to a larger, personal goal or value. Therefore, in order to be motivated to take biz-dev actions, you must know how it will enable you to acquire something that IS valuable to you, such as Income, Invulnerability, Independence, Ideal (way of working), Indulgence, Impact. There are many ways to drive daily actions. For example, check in with a friend daily, be a part of an accountability group, or create a system of points where accumulating points will enable you to "purchase" something positive (a coffee card, vacation time, positive feedback from a leader, etc). Know what you want, keep it front of mind, and track small actions that lead to your goal. You can do it!

93

Resilience. "I've been following your advice and nothing is happening. I want to quit but know

I shouldn't. Help!" Business Development is a "keep on going" activity. If you are contacting people who will need a lawyer at some point, and _if_ you are sending them communications that THEY will find valuable (not a push to engage you) and relevant then you are doing the "right things." Stay with it. You might seek feedback about your communications—do they use a "connective voice?" Are they saying things that fit the needs of the recipient? Is fine tuning needed? Remember, people are busy. You will likely not get the "thank you" response that you want. Quantify your success by whether you are following the biz-dev mantra: the person with the MOST, SUSTAINED, VALUE-BASED relationships makes rain. Your goal is to make relationships. Business will come WHEN they trust you, enjoy knowing you and have a need. Keep assessing what you are doing, manage expectations, and keep taking action. The only "failure" is doing nothing toward your goals.

94

Not good enough. "I am an associate, clearly without the experience of others around me. How can I possibly make a good impression on in-house counsel so I can get business?" The fact that you are thinking about "getting business" as an associate tells me, that you are impressive and "good enough." That distinguishes you. You will show your maturity by the kinds of questions you ask in-house counsel. Showing you know their business and how legal issues impact their goals and directions will leave a positive mark on in-house counsel. Further, offering to assist via relevant introductions (to more experienced lawyers) or sharing information and resources, again puts you in the category of someone they will want to work with at some point. Don't push, brag, or go overboard to attract attention. Start the business development part of your career with small businesses and establishing a track record of great client service, responsiveness, and industry knowledge. Judging yourself as "not good enough" is not productive and likely inaccurate. You are evolving, learning, and gradually taking your position as a mature and capable attorney. Judge yourself with data about accomplishments, not whether someone has selected you from a hugely competitive, mature pool. You will get there!

95

Differences. "My mentor is a 65-year-old man. I watch him schmooz at meetings. That's not me. Does this mean I have to hold my breath and just do it like him?" Absolutely not! Remember, business development is relationship development. In order to foster strong connections, you must be authentic. If you observe that a more "wheeling and dealing, direct style of communicating" doesn't fit you, try a more "searching for similarities, learning about personal aspects, and exploring" style, where you gradually learn where your legal skills might fit into their business. Differences in personality styles are to be expected. Be yourself and maintain an awareness of business. We can all be rainmakers.

96

Dealing with unfamiliar conversations. "I go to events where people often talk about sports. I know nothing about sports and, frankly, don't want to. Do I have to be a sports person in order to be a rainmaker?" I will give you two answers to consider.

1) No, you don't. In the warm-up part of your conversation, you can talk about anything: the city you are in, current events (not controversial), holidays, and, of course, the weather.

2) That being said, the more topics you can talk about, even on the most cursory levels (like headlines you can easily glean from a newspaper), the more versatile you are as a conversationalist. As far as sports are concerned, unless you are adamantly against the topic, just ask, "Do you follow sports?" "What team sports?" "How did they become your favorite?" "How are they doing?" This is enough to touch the topic. Sports, opera, travel, foods—your goal is to engage the other person—topic is not as important as fruitful connection.

97

Momentum. "I haven't closed on a piece of business. Origination credit seems so elusive. How do I know if I am getting there?" Traditionally, business development success has been measured by the end product—an established piece of business. Given the long period it takes to make this happen these days, being discouraged is easy. Lawyers track their time; you know how you are progressing toward your hourly requirement. Do the same thing with business development—track the "small" actions it takes to get to "The O." Research says that it takes 10-20 points of connection for someone to trust you enough to give you a piece of work, when they have a need. Therefore, I suggest that you track actions required to make these connections and sustain relationships. Think one point for an e-mail, telephone call, or brief conversation at a conference. If you set 1000 points a year as your goal you will need to accumulate 84 points a month and four points per work day. That's four brief, valuable e-mails. Tracking your progress gives you the data that say you are creating momentum.

98

Psych-Up. "Here it is, Monday morning. I want to make this a great biz-dev week. How can I get going?" Monday morning starts Sunday night by selecting your goals. Choose an accomplishment that excites you and is realistic. Imagine yourself taking action and being successful. This is what athletes do—they visualize themselves winning. For you, this might be "This is the week 'ABC' Company agrees to move forward on the deal." Think about a way to reach out to them with "Monday Morning Optimism." "Good morning, Leslie. Hope you had a great weekend. As I thought about the project about which we spoke, I had this thought…would welcome talking to you about this as your schedule allows." One action will start your business development race off to a great start. Think positive and remember, judge progress based on your actions, not the response. The more valuable communications you make, the higher the likelihood is that deeper and productive relationships will ensue.

Final Steps

99

Celebrate accomplishments. What lawyers do on a day-to-day basis is monumentally complicated, intense, and exhausting. I hear this in every conversation I have. You are doing what you went to law school to do, and now, something that you didn't see coming (developing business) is required of you in order to succeed. Every action you take to sustain relationships, every time you step out of your comfort zone, every time you carve out 10 minutes to focus on making rain, you are going above and beyond what you learned in law school. Celebrate what you have done. Don't take integrating this "foreign" way of thinking for granted. Sustaining relationships takes time and patience. Track your activities and congratulate yourself for moving in the direction that will enable you to achieve your personal and professional goals.

100

It IS Doable. I've never run a marathon but I know people who have; they research systems to get ready, train, and go. From what I hear it is often painful and there are moments they want to stop—most don't. Apparently, running a marathon is DOable. So is making rain. Just as successful runners do, find a tried and true method that has enabled others to "win," modify it to fit your values, comfort zone and life style, and then implement it consistently. Push through frustrations. You can achieve success in whatever way you define it. Strategy, authenticity, and consistency. Find your unique style and take action no matter what. You CAN make it rain—it IS DOable.

About Karen B. Kahn, EdD PCC

Karen is the Founder and Managing Partner of Threshold Advisors, LLC, a growing "collaborancy™" that focuses on developing talent in the legal industry. She is a professional who answers the request, "tell me something I don't know," with fascinating responses. She lives on the cutting edge of new ideas and is driven to find new ways to solve old problems.

Powered by her knowledge as a psychologist, talent as a certified coach, and respected expertise working with lawyers at various levels and roles, Karen has developed a reputation among law firms and law departments as the "go-to" person to generate success in the ever-changing world of being an attorney.

The expanse of her work is vast and includes speaking, consulting and coaching topics such as strategic business development; implementing collaboration to foster internal and external valuable relationships; building/strengthening gender initiatives; expanding the impact of affinity groups; creating successful industry groups; and strategic-advancement training and coaching. Personally and professionally, she is a strong believer and implementer of the people-helping-people philosophy; she practices what she teaches (and coaches). Whether delivering a program/seminar, consulting with a law firm, or coaching attorneys, Karen seeks to be a valuable, active contributor. Her belief in inclusivity, the power of community, operating with a clear vision, and strong sense of purpose allows her to help organizations take action toward developing cultures where individuals stay and succeed. She accomplishes these goals in one-on-one, group, and workshop formats, as well as through organizational collaboration and consulting.

Presenting for organizations including the National Association of Women Lawyers, Legal Marketing Association, National Association of Law Placement and individual law firm retreats, provides Karen the vehicles she loves to share ideas and encourage success.

Before founding Threshold Advisors, Karen maintained a successful private coaching/psychology practice. She also established herself as a thought leader through her activities as a university professor, author, and developer/leader of more than 1000 seminars and workshops.

Karen earned her doctoral degree in psychology from the University of Virginia in 1977, followed by an internship at The Ohio State University. She received a B.A. with honors from Trinity College in Connecticut in 1973.

Currently, Karen happily resides on the beach in Westport, Connecticut, from which she frequently commutes to New York City. Spending time with family, friends and her two golden retrievers and pocket boxer, and basking in the excitement of her children who are following their passions, brings smiles to her face.

Always Happy to Chat

Beginnings start with conversations. I welcome the chance to hear about your goals, "I would love tos," challenges, and opportunities. The legal profession is changing. If you or your firm is standing at the threshold of new directions, ideas, and models, I would love to talk, listen, encourage, and help.

Contact me at: Karen@ThresholdAdvisors.com

It IS Doable… one step at a time.

Making Rain is a "Small" Deal

It is a series of small daily actions, in many ways just like other behaviors in your life, that can be woven into small pockets of time and even into the typical flow of your personal and professional pursuits. The keys are to implement smart (time respecting) approaches, utilize your own, natural way of developing relationships and integrate a constant awareness of other people's personal and professional needs into your conversations.

Daunting to DOable helps lawyers understand that they **can** develop the relationships and business required to succeed in whatever way each defines it, and, in fact, when done authentically and naturally, making rain can actually be fun.

Available on Amazon and other online bookstores.

Interested in sharing this with your firm?
Quantity orders for both *Daunting to DOable* and 1*00 Steps to DOable* are available at significant discounts. Contact the author at Karen@ThresholdAdvisors.com for details.

Made in the USA
Lexington, KY
20 December 2019

58893172R00066